去动物园

Early Literacy Series : Level C

Copyright © 2022 by Level Learning, INC.

All rights reserved. No part of this book may be reproduced in any form or by any electronic or mechanical means without permission in writing from the publisher.

ISBN 978-1-64040-141-9

Content by Jingyao Qi
Illustration by Matt Austin

Published by Level Learning, INC.

About Level Learning:

Level Learning provides a Chinese literacy focused curriculum for K-12 classrooms. Our data driven literacy system allows teachers to better understand and more accurately assess the development of student's literacy. Our program includes 40 levels of Language Skills, Reading Skills and Book Leveling for fiction and non-fiction, as well as formative online assessments and data analytics to inform instruction.

To learn more about our entire offering, visit www.levellearning.com

About Level Learning Early Literacy Offering:

Level Learning Early Literacy offering provides a structured and systematic approach to teaching the most commonly used Chinese characters to new learners. Our offering teaches characters through story-telling and themes that are familiar to young learners.

Level Learning provides two unique Early Literacy offering – 1) book series and 2) assessment and tracking system.

Book Series include:
- 12 leveled books across levels A through D
- Games for students to practice what they've learned
- Teachers' guide with stories and key teaching points to help teach characters in the context of a story

To download games and teacher's guide, visit www.levellearning.com

Assessment and Tracking system is available as part of Level Learning subscription and provides mastery-based online assessment and data analytics for every level to show student's learning progress and gap. To start a subscription, contact support@levellearning.com.

这是一只小狗。

狗

一 狗

这是一只小猫。

猫

一 猫

这是一只小鸡。

鸡

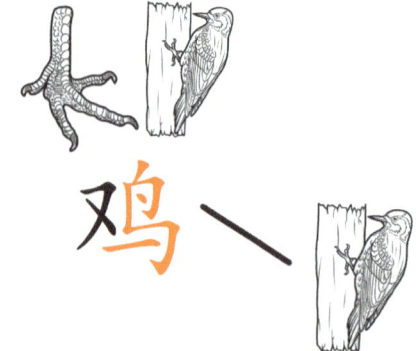

鸡

这是一只小鸭。

鸭

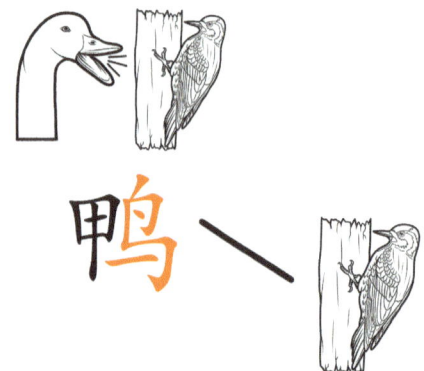

这是一只小鸟。

鸟

鸟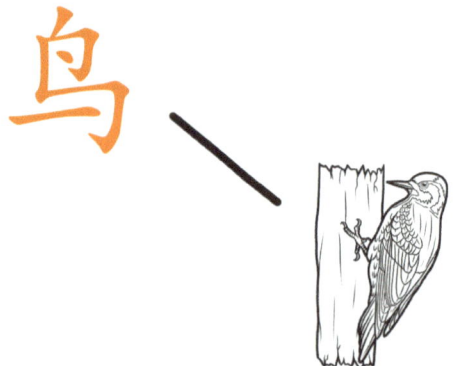

这是一只蝴蝶。

蝴蝶

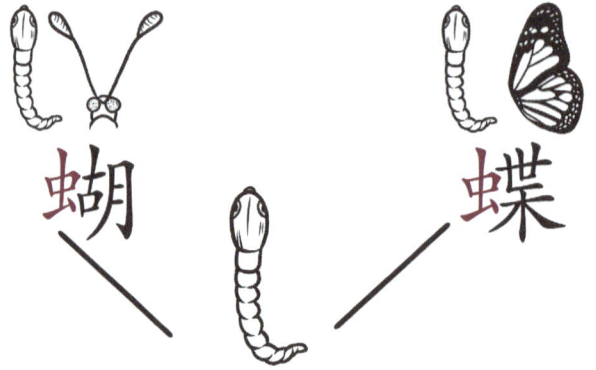
蝴　蝶

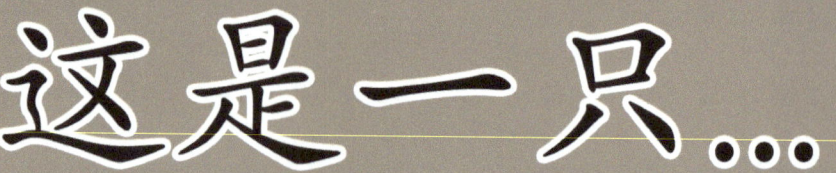

这是一只猴子。

猴

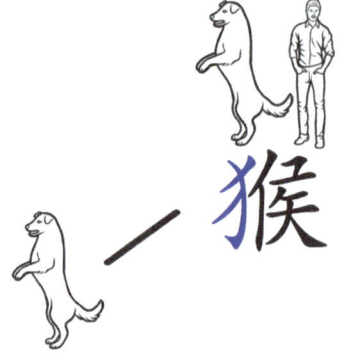

跑

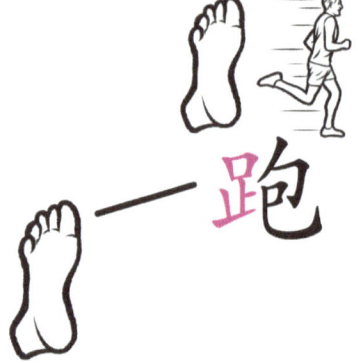

这是一只狮子。

狮

快跑啊!

www.ingramcontent.com/pod-product-compliance
Lightning Source LLC
Chambersburg PA
CBHW041122070526
44584CB00002B/248